FAULT

Also by Katharine Coles

Fire Season
The Golden Days of the Fourth Dimension
History of the Garden
The Measurable World
The One Right Touch

FAULT

poetry

Katharine Coles

RED HEN PRESS | Los Angeles, California

Fault

Book design by Mark E. Cull
Layout assistance by Claudia Avalos

Cover image: John Clerk of Eldin's 1795 engraving of unconformities,
from James Hutton's *Theory of the Earth*
Courtesy of Rare Books Division
Special Collections
J. Willard Marriott Library
University of Utah

ISBN: 978-1-59709-390-3
Library of Congress Catalog Card Number: 2008928467

The California Arts Council and the National Endowment for the Arts partially support Red Hen Press.

Red Hen Press
www.redhen.org

First Edition

For my brothers, Jeffrey and Peter Coles—
luck, and the good eye to see it when it comes.

Acknowledgments

Grateful acknowledgement to the following journals in which these poems have appeared: *Antioch Review:* "Anthropomorphism"; *Ascent:* "The Anatomist"; "Anatomical Theater," "Fault," "Kepler's Paradoxes," "Middle Ages"; *Barrow Street:* "On the Beagle"; *The Colorado Review:* "The Practice of Hunger," "Good Eye"; *The Paris Review:* "Unproved Pantoum," "Lines Taken From a Poem on Luck, Unwritten," "The Botanical Gardens"; *Petroglyph:* "Marriage: The Wheel," "Canyon Ghazal"; *Poetry:* "A Confusion," "The Double Leash"; *A Smartish Pace:* "Hotel Orologio," "The Numbers"; *Western Humanities Review:* "Marriage: Ghazal," "Outside Newton's House," "The Salt City"; and to the following anthologies: *Girl's Best Friend:* "A Confusion" (reprint); *Ravishing Disunities:* "Marriage: Ghazal" (reprint), "Canyon Ghazal" (reprint).

"The Numbers" appears as part of a permanent installation by visual artist Anna Campbell Bliss in the Leroy Cowles Mathematics Building on the University of Utah Campus. "A Confusion," "The Double Leash," "Fault," "Marriage: Ghazal," and "Middle Ages" appeared in *Natural Histories*, part of an ongoing collaboration with visual artist Maureen O'Hara Ure that resulted in an installation of words and images in the Salt Lake Art Center in 1998. "Lament" was first published by the Galleria Venezia Viva, Venice, in a limited edition artist's book, *Lament*, with original collages by Bruno Blenner.

"After Fever" was set for voice and orchestra by composer Steve Roens, and premiered in February 2008 as part of his *Specific Gravity*, a larger setting of poems by the author.

"Accidental," "Picking Blackberries," "The Double Leash," "After Fever," "The Anatomist," "Canyon Ghazal," and "Poetry and Spirituality" were originally written for the anthology *A Year In Place*, edited by W. Scott Olsen and Brett Lott and published by the University of Utah Press.

The author is grateful for the support of the University of Utah Faculty Research Committee, which provided the generous travel grant that resulted in "Good Eye," in "Kepler's Paradoxes," and in the poems in the *Alchemy* sequence.

Last and most, she is grateful to friends and others who took the time to read and comment on this manuscript and individual poems in it, especially David Baker, Karen Brennan, Kenneth Brewer, Kevin Cantwell, Michael Collier, Richard Howard, Scott Olsen, Peggy Shumaker and Melanie Rae Thon.

Contents

III. Alchemy

I. Accidental

On the Beagle

Even there, time
Won't stop plowing the dark—in the lash

Fluttering your cheek; in the swallow,
The catch in the throat; in your hand lifting—

A constant wind drives through you.
Even if you could sit completely still
You could not stop. Imagine the billowed sails;

Pace the deck, mind adrift on time.
Say you could slow your breathing to mere memory

Of breath, could stop your heart and your heart's echo,
Time would keep ticking through your cells—
Past the instant breath did not return

And the pulse split its infinitive
Into the future, which belongs to others,

Your body's issue growing out of proportion,
And into the cells of what feeds on you:

Minute, voracious mouths grazing your skin,
Harvest returning you to the relentless present
Each cell turns over wave by wave

Into new business, some other occupation,
Another dust-up, another blow to the heart.

Good Eye

1. A luminous thing: the clock, unglassed, seen
First time in over three decades,
Since I was seven. Mere opening
Of pupil into the dark, and time's face
Presents itself. Even now, too often
I close my eyes to see, and forget
To open them, feeling my way by hand
Through the familiar dark. Even now the light
Has blazed across my eyes, sharp, to sharpen
Them back into unaided vision, I must
Remind my brain to use them. *See, waken,*
It thinks again, every moment just
Turning outward, composing the usual room
From light, not memory; the real from dream.

2. Imagine perfect symmetry. Gone, a universe,
To rough edges, galaxies on the fly.
Admit: nowadays, looking at the sky,
We don't look. We plant fields of ears
The scientist turns on her great, grinding gears—
And on our dollar—heaven's way,
Toward those resonant flame spheres whirring by,
Lost in burning themselves out. Sheer
Suicides. Once we've considered them, there.
If one snuffs out before the machine sees it
Did it exist? Still matter, that distant sign
Screened, translated, already so determined
She can barely distinguish it from static,
The cosmic mumble messing up the line.

3. I've been visiting old observatories
Wound around their stairs, so much glass
Set in stone that spins itself by stories
Into sky. How those dead men must
Have loved their nightly flights, the polished plates
That flung them heavenward in fire and gas.
They made our universe. Some nights
Surely they remembered just to gaze,
Instead, say, of counting—all those points!—
Or measuring the arc from star to star,
And, by measuring, fixing it. Just there,
Spaced by minutes and seconds.
What it's taken us to travel here.
We count our time by spinning round a star.

4. So: happiness. I think all the time
Of luck. Once, I raised my eyes to see
A flock of southbound geese inscribe the moon:
V for virtue, voracious, velocity's
Swift kick to the ribs, for the flight
Of beating ghosts, for geese wheeling
To their private star, some small light
Only they can read by. How do they feel it?
A signal on the brain, in the heart—
Call it lodestar, magnet, pulling them
Across the helpless heavens. I've no such art,
No sure sign how to travel home.
So I wander, happy. And why not?
How lost can I be? My tiny planet?

5. By such measurements we are blessed.
Safety in numbers: force on an airplane's wing;
Centuries ago, a ship was placed at last
In time and so in space. The spheres sing,
As does the laser, counting its cut, precise
So I, too, will see by the numbers,
Cornea peeling, slice by measured slice.
Two months later, I almost can't remember
What it was like not to see. So pure—
What the physicist sees—she must imagine
It in equations to make it visible. There,
Not only in some numeric heaven
Ghosted by ideas. Machines click on,
Counting on the ever-divisible photon.

6. Sometimes, I can hardly remember which stairs
Turned into which night, which window
Overlooked what city, its luminous glow
Reflected from which flow of river
Some ancient instruments lifted my gaze above.
We all think ourselves symmetrical,
Even touching our hearts. *Now, now,*
We know so much more than we can see. All
We've ever known. And luck: do we
Use it or use it up? My cup's full
To brimming in the moment I drain it dry,
And if it had a brim, the sky would spill
Over its own edges. Violent spark
Is all that burns the blood through the heart.

7. Our universe, cold and broken. Wonderful,
To live even in restless peace like this:
My city torn by whirlwind, the cloud funneled
By earth's turn overhead. Such a noise
Of wind's engine, the future the engine bears.
In flying machines, we tend oracles
We count on for warning. No sign here
Until heaven had turned all wrack, all
Ruin.
          But not all ruin.
                                        Catastrophe
Builds in the future's darkness. What's left. *Not all.*
Across the ocean, fault will turn a city:
Shaken, it undoes us, wall by wall.
Number human against human, wave, or fire.
Too many dead to count. So I count stars

8. Cresting into the future through my glass walls.
They too are unaccountable, and will die—
Glimmering planets, the drama of these falls
Of heaven into my time. The past looks so light.
The tornado didn't take a single leaf
From my branches, though neighbors lost roofs, trees
Planted forty years ago. No real ease
Anywhere on earth. I find, out back,
Shingles, guttering, glass. An architect's dream
Of shelter sailed, drafted lines intact,
Miles on wind's twist around its eye.
So clear. *Another breath, another day.*
Short on miracles, what else can I do
But count them down to measure my long luck.

1999, Padova, Paris, Greenwich, Salt Lake City, Izmit

Lines Taken from a Poem on Luck, Unwritten

Aix-les-Bains

After the curistes are all evacuated, from my balcony I watch
the hotel next-door burn down.

Water. Man. The fire burns all night.
The body burns its own flesh back to blazes.
What to cheer for? Darkness, or the light
Drawn down from heaven? *That* touch mesmerizes.

The body burns its own flesh back to blazes.
So near the fire, I'm cold. *Elaborate*:
Drawn down from heaven, what touch mesmerizes?
Moves to still me? Too early or too late,

Too near the fire. *I'm cold.* Elaborate,
The dance makes its own music, all its own
Moves. *Still me.* Too early or too late,
Something I've called shelter is undone.

The dance makes its own music all its own.
What's left me in the morning? Emptiness,
Something I've called shelter. *I'm undone*,
And I've only watched, just blown the kiss.

Leave me in the morning. Emptiness,
Blue sky. Spoiled, even flame lies down,
But I have only watched. Just blown, the kiss
Flies like roof to ash. *Like time.* My own

Blue sky unspoiled. *Even flame lies down.*
What to hope for: darkness or—? Made light,
Roof flies to ash, but not this time my own.
Water. Fire. *Man, it burned all night.*

2000

And why shouldn't it be arbitrary?
Balance, cause-effect, truth. This
Catch in the throat, the blown kiss.
Every headline's an obituary

For what we've set aside—a thousand years
Blown with last night's rockets into heaven—
And if it is two thousand, the year is gone
Before it's started, days not even numbered

But oddly disappeared, like so many
Of our century's faces. Into steel
And concrete. Into blood. Under the heel
Of one boot or another. Imagine a skinny

Kid whose mother vanished into passion,
The child left suspended in the change:
This lost year, this mystery, this hinge
Between the past and a future we insist on

Entering before its time. A time is gone
But it's not finished. Who could blame us
For wanting to turn our back on it, its fuss
And detail, its specificity and bone-

Dry arguments. The trouble with the past:
It's full of facts. The future's something else,
General, prettily hazed, all its quarrels
Unarticulated, sure not to last

From one day to another. Is it dawn
Or just the light of snow that stripes the blankets?
We are warm. The year a blank. Yet
I can't stop worrying the millennium,

Details already abstracted into *violence*—
Whatever so angered us, the all-
Or-nothing reel of rage. Dawn's fall
Down light's perfect pitch. A darkened voice.

The Royal Armouries

September 20, 2001; Tower of London; Leeds

Unhewn rock. The sling David holds
Balanced with such grace in marbled hand—

All history: the history of war—
All over the world. Longbow. Sword.

The queen has so many blades she's divided them.
It all happened earlier in China: their crossbow shot
While we primitives sharpened sticks; their firelance

While we were pouring hot oil from our ramparts.
The history of war: the history of technology.
The middle ages: one vast hallucination,

Points kept honed and glinting for centuries.
The Arabs wrote out recipes for gunpowder.

Then, in 1850, our machine gun.
Revolving rifle: 1855.
You've noticed, haven't you, how we speed up

Time, so only now can we see clearly?
The history of technology, the history of beauty,

And therefore of loss. No more dragon's-head hammers,
Inlays of angels, unicorns, fantastic

Wing-shouldered griffins contorting haft and barrel.
Only clear sight. No more luck,
Art and the uncertain human touch

To carry the aim astray—all give way
First to the semi-automatic,
Then to gas and wing, invisible fallout

Defining its target so fully with its drift
We call it accurate. We always thought

Beauty might be fatal, its history
History's only end. Outside the museum

Light nicks and glances off the river.
In here, it catches blades arrayed

As if they were forged to turn the sun for us.
Someone imagined this hall. Placed the windows

To bring us to the bearing edge of grief.
River. Desert. The world moves us all
Equally toward the moment we're suspended

To take our last plunge into winter.
A matter now of keyboards, maps, and code.
On the other side of the world, already tomorrow,

A field blooming hard. Late poppies open
(To their last good chance, to our sun)

So deep in history we can't imagine.
Just there, our spear plants its chiseled head.

The Practice of Hunger

1. Not absence. No more empty
than space, which curves, fills, grows into its own

weight and satisfaction: the body carved out
of element, until
muscle and bone are taken, then

blood. What I have to give him,
                                    though I eat
everything he brings: rich truffles, breads
stuffed with fruits so jeweled

their sweetness breaks on my teeth, flesh
red at center and bright with fat

that scorches through me, all
burning itself to ash. What

remains: residue
of privilege, speed, desire's
revved engine. Solstice

darkens into its moment, and I can't help
any of this melting into hunger
he keeps feeding.

2.   Not for us

city's nighttime alleys, cans
set by back doors, what we've refused

ripening into hand. Not the lettered sign,
the man we hardly see at curbside
whose two dogs, moist eyes rolled up,

arrest our eyes. Not those deserts
creeping over lands across the oceans, seed

ground to dust, dust illuminated by the remote
span of our late attention: mothers
wrapping children turning first to eye

and skull, the brain's determined house,
then, under the lenses' neutral force,
to static

3.   dreaming
the world's end. Any form: caps
melting under sun's barrage; particles

too small to see chipping away at nothing
more than air, the skin's veneer, all rendered

graph and chart on the evening news. Any wave
building far from shore. Maybe not

a cataclysm we would open arms to: flame
roiling from an angry eye, plates
shifting, as if to wake, under houses

shaken to dust. Right now, on all sides, stars
fold and unfold around their deaths,

shedding fire, the atom
fractured into brilliancy.
                              Or simple erosion.
                                        Some charms

4. we've always lived by. If I believed,
I might have taken a vow, the cloth

from any hand, the table
spread with linen, its objects chipping
the air with light. Might

have shorn myself of ornament, all history
frozen in lapis and topaz, silk's whispering

about the body's motion; shorn
myself even of naked weight, that luxury

the hand presses, then the lip,
pleasure's arch vaulting back through

brain's dim cathedral. How the mouth,
even taking the polished cup, smears,
taught by blood to speak

strenuous denial, the clappered tongue
telling over its stark, resonant *no*.

Fault

After John Clerk of Eldin's 1795 engraving of Hutton's geologic
unconformity, as reproduced in *Time's Arrow, Time's Cycle* by
Stephen Jay Gould.

*. . .[U]nconformities are palpable proof that the earth does not
decline but once into ruin.*

—Stephen Jay Gould

What I know about time is
minute: the mineral taste of his skin
dissolving, the interval of a sparrow's eye, phlox

and orange lilies setting summer to rest
in fire and wind. His fear of heights

grounds us. During its winter sleep,
the garden grows a new crop of rocks
we dig all spring. In the engraving,

provisional lines of fence and hedgerow
tame the field: two men believe earth keeps

still under the phaeton's rolling wheels
and their horses paw a ground

weightier than this friable shell of dust
smoothing history's flotsam over. Since then,
we've learned distrust for everything

that holds us. In fragile scratches,
the engraver undercuts the world
they know, heaves it beneath their feet, an ocean

eating its skim of ice. In its own sweet time
the land founders. Hutton, the first to set
his foot on that uneasy surface, must have thought
Don't look down. Looking, I want

to walk right to the edge, the life I inhabit
a shell I contain. His hand on the pillow
open, his hand closed. Even the window flows,

subject to gravity's tides. How distant from
each other we travel, bedded together,
eyelids flickering as if, beneath their skins,

buried ground were stirring, taking flight
into our deepest sleep, into our waking.

Hotel Orologio

Bologna

The calendar is intolerable to all wisdom, the horror of all astronomy,
and a laughing-stock from a mathematician's point of view.

—Francis Bacon

1. *Incipit.* The argument of moon and sun
Contradicting each other by long degrees;
Months and seconds of a marriage, lunatic

As any, across which the body
Draws pulse and shadow; mass

Against whose pull we tilt and bobble—
But meantime, I rise alone in a hotel

2. Named for the space between us. A wake-up call,
Though the room hums with time's devices:
Electric calendar, electric clock

That's lost its hands but buzzes through the minutes,
Counting invisibly from the desk
While the nightstand clock flips its digits

And the TV maps the weather. Six-fifteen.
3. You would like this room's machined noise,
Though the postcard will reach you after I do:

The tower clock. In the window, its face turns
Right to me. I even have a scale
So I can count in kilos how I've passed

Time in Italy, bean by tender bean. Each second
Something lodges under the skin.
    4. Days will shorten. We'll take our time to notice.

And will I notice, if I lose a day
Moon, sun, and stars can't reconcile?
Here is what comes of division:

Eleven minutes here and there add up.
In prison half a life, I'd think of time
But only how it left me, not the numbers
    5. That might help me keep it all in mind—

And Bacon won in time, though never
Soon enough to know it. For all this,

We have too many instruments to mismeasure
The universe's raucous goings-on
By swoops and dips, unlikely spheres turning

Heaven's great gestures overhead:
    6. The stars have always moved us to miscount

Intervals, daylight hours, clever turns, as if
Geometry could elaborate truth from vision,
Globes imagined with such intricate love

They show the power of mind over matter—
Mind winged or windblown, toothed, nailed
To some mast overlooking sea

7. Monsters, muscle-bound gods, serpents coiled
To guard our progress from the unknown: oh,

The mind can encompass any world
It creates, down to the peacock tail

Spread to fan a mystic continent,
World turning over in such a prison
Of belabored metal, orbit, transit,

8. Only mind, that stubborn, matterless thing,
Wrong-headed, could free us, set us drifting
On the rolling, nothing wave of time

Then measure a second to the quadrillionth.
Clocking fire. Explosions. Music. Shadows.
Angles and rolling balls, spheres dropping,

Stone, cesium atoms, crystals, fans.
9. And I could go on—though sand, in its way,

Is more like it, that wave of particles,
Or the movement of shadow across a face.
Even aroma: the ember burning down

This incense stick to ash, thread by thread, until
The steel ball dips. Time's up. Truth, after all,

Is only time, though there is beauty in it
10. Until we try to parse it—the second now

Marked and packeted, a discretion
That never was until we imagined it.

This is what comes of mathematics:
The equinox slides its way into midsummer.
Whatever we try to measure, we count wrong.

The truth: it's hot in Italy, solstice gone
     11. To heat. Where you sleep, it's still spring:
The earth whirling you headlong into summer

Carries me away from you just as fast.
At dinner, I'll eat fresh tomatoes

Spilling seed and liquid, perfected moment.
Artichokes. Oil pressed from olives

Harvested last fall. I'm a tourist,
     12. Only passing through. Traveling alone,
I will drop my eyes from strangers' eyes

As if the gaze could create force between us,
Light, particular. I could count the days
Without you, but numbers cannot alter

What the body knows. I ride its wave,
Cresting before we know it.
                   Not explicit.

Accidental

1. I move into it
     and the world solidifies—

scorched hill giving to cool
     range, tree to forest—

and keeps giving.
     The way I hold

the expected note
     against its shift,

a kind of ghost,
     in the space between them

a life's sweet pain.
     All horizon,

this dawn I run through,
     summer falling into

afternoon, when he, still
     now sleeping,

will pump his bike
     up this same canyon

while I sit dreaming frescoes
     on ancient walls, colors

brushed white by time's
      long flutter of wings,

walls I walked through, standing
      as if surprised

to find themselves supporting
      no roof, no attic,

no portrait or rack for hanging
      spoons and crockery over

space the archaeologist believes
      burned under food

as if to hurry time.

2.   About which we say, *Done.*

Through which water
      still flows

and fire tears, air
      eroding under

that stream giving up
      stillness, leaving

disaster's ghost
      etched on the walls,

no more. Smoke
        pours out windows, empties

into nothing, knots
        my chest. So close

my mind still bellies
        all night under

smoke, pulls
        the plug, turns

the water on, passes
        on danger—while,

3. across a continent, an ocean, fingers
        touched wires, set

the timer, so
        intentional, so gentle, their

precision looked
        like nothing

so much as love, until
        wall came down, floor on floor

collapsed like time;
        until the shoppers, militiamen taking

days off, mothers with strollers
    stepped into that

separate
    space a moment

dismembered, silence
    holding, held

as if dust could stop
    its flight, until the mouth

opened, the first
    scream entering time.

4. Millennia later. The second
    before. I'm still beating

against the world as if it mattered,
    shaking my hair

free of those wings as if
    I could, as he shakes off

the bee—lazed
    coincidence of flight

he's wheeled into—
    and in one gesture's

passing irritation enters
time's slant

skid
sideways, wheels holding

his weight it seems forever, then
wheel folding;

and even as he tells me how
he got us

here, into emergency,
my mind slips

his words, grasps
how space folds—

moment's comprehension,
the way a bird's color

flutters the eye,
mind never

composing it into *bird.* Then gone;
the head

meeting asphalt
in that moment

thinks, *Gone. I knew this
was coming.*

5.   Blood.

Flash of green and light
        estranged by chemical

wash, long adrenalin surge
        toward the wail.

*I almost had
        control*, he says later. I almost

had it, under
        doctor's hands seaming

flesh over bone.
            How many stitches?

I ask, but I think
        emergency room, as if it made

its own space, as if my mind
        could hold one thing,

my lucky life of near
        misses and their ghosts,

and he says
        I almost had it

and I hold his hand, wondering how
　　　to get the blood

from his long hair,
　　　his favorite green shirt,

trying not to picture
　　　earth's dizzy

flash of spoke, how
　　　soft is bone and tissue

he carries his life in,
　　　its matter lately

divided, abstracted by numbers,
　　　bits so minute

they dissolve even my love into
　　　mere idea (his so

solid shoulder, blood
　　　on my hand), and I

can no more
　　　imagine them than

infinity. Which
　　　they contain.

Late summer, 1998

II. THE DOUBLE LEASH

Lament

One day his heart unraveled—oh!—my own.
I pulled the thread myself, my blue undoing.
What do I do now? These empty rooms—
I who let the wind scour them clean.

He pulled the thread himself, his blues undoing.
The world becomes enough, light and blue
I have let the wind scour clean.
Sometimes, his heart closed so hard

The world became enough. *Light. Blue
Thread undone.* So light sews the world.
Sometimes, my heart opens so hard
It pulls the world in and won't let go

Its thread.
             My light's undone.
                              So goes the world.
What do I do now? These empty rooms
Pull the world in and won't let go.
One day his heart unraveled. *Oh, my own.*

Marriage: Ghazal

What's lost in love? What retrieved? It could be
we lose ourselves to make love what could be.

He offers water, but I want to burn
the night down. I ask where the Glenlivet could be.

Night tricks from its air cloth he slips into.
Does he keep just arms up those sleeves? That *could* be.

Eye of grosgrain, button of palest shell
hanging on thread's delicate *could be*.

My spine shivers open along the zipper's teeth:
the touch withheld, air softer than velvet could be.

He unfastens darkness, unhooks it down to skin—
he never knew how elusive light could be.

His is the hand that undoes me at last.
His undoing's all I conceived night could be.

As pearl is to mother, mortal heart to cage,
grain's nubbins are to the sheaves: what could be.

Even the most fragile bud troubles forth,
caught open early, to bear the bright, cold bee.

Touch of a thief on a tiny catch. I'm sprung,
taken by promise's predicate: could be.

What have I got? Words to undo the heart with
a wink and a whisper: *It is, Sweet,* not *Love, it could be.*

Marriage: Little Bell

I can't help it. So I travel
miles at a touch. Blood ravels
blue roads adrift under the veil

of early mystery. See, how I'm enthralled
touching tongue to words? In thrall
to your syllable in my ear. All

small, soft mammal, pulsed fur, quarry
to your baying. Oh, don't worry—
I would not betray you, go awry,

blame you here. Call you *rascal,
ordinary mortal, heaven, love.* Your skull
grown readable in my hand. I cull

all I can from touch: good and ill, babble
of names in your blood, your able
tongue ringing me, little bell's

clapper, into song—oh, *innocent
nameless,* we are no longer, if we were, nascent
flesh, aglow. I wouldn't give a cent,

now, to hear the dull confession
making you love's own airy scion,
enraptured into *myth, atomic glow, charged ion*

escaping my sphere. Don't disclose
any more. Just come close,
here. I hold all I have to lose,

still no Helen, peril's beauty, truant
face made bold to lead us into ruin.
Weakling. My own heart could do me in.

Marriage: The Wheel

Neither prison nor respite. No asylum.
If I'm pure rose, I draw you up through xylem
into dream. Rooted in you. Bloody, um-

bilical.
      Nothing in me
          of flower's
perfume. Nor of patience. Hand over hand, I lower
myself into the waiting. Every hour

blooms into its chamber, little terror
of bees. Do not make me sit, tell each error
over, stung, strung bead, finger, or

knotted tic in some precise, binary
mind, counting ones and twos. Nary
an explosion. I'm for any other airy

dreamworld.
      Sorry.
         Again
            I've gone Medieval,
lost perspective, flattened: little devil
of the machine, millennium's feted, ill-

got girl bound. Science, history, neurotic
to the core, catherine wheel and switch gone erotic
under some newfangled touch.
          Bitch.
            Just skin.
              Tick

of muscle, clenched hand, every sinew
glinting, electricity remade, so new
it binds each heartbeat: you, and you, and you.

Marriage: Last Case

I'm not writing, this time, to scold,
to complain about my bones. The cold
sets in, yes—but I want to grow old

like this, toughening, no elegance
but also no regret, no backward glance
at some encumbered beauty; no spoon or lance,

paraphernalia of decline. Sedative
just blunts loss's edge; declension (nominative, dative)
is, worst case, just tense. No mere tiff,

no bitter end. Confess: you are no Pharoah
sailing me to the tomb, no Romeo, no harrow
to my field, nor, to my Psyche, Eros—

or is it *arrows*, this piercing—bulb's filament
trembling light. To my grief, lament.
None of this was ever what you meant,

and think how you've got off. The heart's insurgent
after all, and no mere surgeon
can cut out what fails. The pulse, urgent,

beats me toward you still, insensible
to return, its close chamber. *Be sensible*—
but your lips pressed my palm. *They did.* No Sybil

I; just, next century, your stern daguerre-
otype, light between your fingers. *C'est la guerre*,
you'll tell yourself at night. *Tell the air.*

A Confusion

Not even a decent pack. Just a pair,
though in small rooms they move to multiply.
A piebald dog. A dog with golden fur.
One who herds. One who gulps each fly
that buzzes her, cracking it in snap jaws.
Tonight, stretched out on oriental rugs,
a relaxation of dogs, dog tired; a doze
and snoring. Then absolution: a bliss of dogs,
a conflagration, a swarm, unspooled. Odd
dogs, chasing the invisible. Like me. A fool,
a blaze of dogs, a plight, an inspiration
of frenzied tongue and paw; two dogs in a pod,
mathematic. An education. Love's school
in wilderness, its muzzled exultation.

The Double Leash

Blizzard to lilac. Dandelion
to leaf. Endless
variation of seasons I note

in passing, smells
I cannot smell: rotting
gardens, feces, musk of cat.
                        These two

run in front of me, golden
shoulder to patchwork, heads
lifted or lowered into

scent, tongues lolling. Ears
damp with their own
spittle and each other's

tell me, tethered a pace behind,
their journey's epic: tipping
forward to the familiar or
stranger's distant yap; angling

to my breathing, whispered
praise, my slightest
suggestion.
                Ignored.
                      The shepherd
throws herself into

any whirring wheel, to herd
the neighbor's tractor mower or
the UPS truck's packets
home; pulling her back,

the golden's oblivious
ballast, instinct heading
always for the gutter's

deepest puddle, her own way
within the forked leash's
one-foot range. As we pass,

the clans set up
their barking, as if we
were news, gathering center

of a congenial warning
din—mine answer with
disturbances of pace, an extra pull
or lollop, grins thrown

slant-eyed over shoulders
until one hears a call
she can't ignore, surrenders

to baying's ferocious
joy moving
muscle and bone. Moving
storm, storm's eye: happy

universes whirl in their skins
as I do in mine. Unknowable,
their fate. Mediums between
foreign principalities, they're tied

to me, to each other, by my will,
by love; to that other realm
by song, and tooth, and blood.

After Fever

Under his bush,
invisibly, the grouse
folds his wings, won't flush;

in a week, hoppers
have taken over the grass,
as if they'd waited for

my eyes to turn away.
My step, tentative, still
springs them into flight,

crazy, sideways, light
bodies flung toward
they can't know what

fortune of leaf or flower,
water or pavement's disaster.
They take their chance

as I do, too soon
climbing blue spectacle,
a perfect breeze, out

of body's consumption. How
invisible well-being, worn
like lightest cloth

the wind moves, sheer
exhiliration, over
skin, the world alight

as I come back to it—
how pain is felt
as presence, not the slipping

away from one's own—
the terrible body's weight,
its knowledge, burning out.

Poetry & Spirituality

Today, the wind rides the thighs of grasshoppers,
and leaves fly like rescue from burning trees
I could almost turn into something. All this talk.

I'm guilty too—me, an unbeliever
raising a miracle, these ungainly hoppers
pelting my chest, my hips, fixing a moment

to my shorts, my footfall opening one
so brilliantly into flight you might think
butterfly, before its wings let it down.

Picking Blackberries

Noon. Hottest
day turning into
hazed cloister. I eat

fruit gone too far
wild for love's table: deep

gone into ripening's
doze, lopsided, grown
odd-bodied, estranged, but

so sweet, lateness
broken on the tongue.
Where is that

perfected body I keep
reaching under leaf

and thorn to pick? He
dreams on, asail before
the bedroom's machined breeze.

I'm still eating, finding
no berry fine
enough to feed him.

Canyon Ghazal

They fall against their rising, cliffs undone
by weather and what weather's left undone.

Sunk at canyon bottom, the road scales
its arched body into lift undone.

And I run within a thunder's pulse
that lights me through, flickering off and on.

What haven't I done? Wind strips the oaks. Limbs
strain at root, by their wild heft undone.

Even the sky can't stop. It gnaws itself,
black cloud undone by black, unloosened one.

What can I do but let the storm trouble
eye and blood, the heart at wrist undone?

Until it's passed, moving me between
nerve and fault. I resist. Undone,

the coal's consumed by its own breath. No rain.
Just trembling air. Sky's whip. The passion done.

Anthropomorphism

The dogs come in, all joy, shivering
Uncollared air like fear from their skins.

We own the neons, alight behind that glass
As if they flew. They look back at us.

We cartoon moose upended, cap the squirrel
Sidekick, unflappable, ever over a barrel

Or doing unto others what we'd like to:
Bird decliffs coyote, or takes a beak to—

Over stomach and twitch, project that film,
Reeled story uncompacting the unknown.

Today, even the hawk, ferocious, rebuilding,
Crosses sky with twig and string. Unstrung,

Each body's flight's an x. I haven't seen
It any spring but this. It hasn't been

Like me to see. Sky and desire.
Tree-crotch, down, terror. No stranger

To such need, the broken-open heart
Flutters its wings. *Home. Small comfort.*

The Botanical Gardens

And consider the way they are always in progress,
Even after centuries; the way they hide
The speaker but not the voice. The sound

Of water falling. *Over there.* The way
These flowers warn us not to eat them

By color and smell. The labels have to tell us,
Spidering faded letters under the leaves.
Sometimes we take our chances. Sometimes

We're right. The way we're given to nature;
The way we swallow down the new, ripe fruit.
The way we defy nature, given to hope,

Making of stem and leaf what we will.
The way stem and leaf remake our will.

For example, the way we see ourselves
In these flesh-eating plants and are afraid—this,

So like a toothy fiddlehead, red flowers curling
(How color attracts as lief as warns),
Each little hanging chamber modeled to tempt

Any small life into its shade,
Driven by its own hunger to consummation.

We are far too big to be taken in.
The way we stand and watch. Where's the danger?
Under these canopies? Deep in the green throat?

The Salt City

As if all of them—not only a wife, a mother, singular,
        but all the wives and mothers, and also
sons and uncles, daughters, family spaniels,
            sisters, fathers, kick-abouts, the stray cockatiel—
                have turned to what they fled, they become

transfigured, mute and gleaming under a harsh,
        evaporative light that chastens even
the salt-dry shrubs of August, already tindered
        foothills, skyscrapers (so lately just
            reflective, raised from fired sheets of sand

and unrevealing), the marbled halls of government,
        Ford Explorers, distant peaks. Would-be vagrants cast
glancing over half-turned shoulders, not
        regretful, nor compassionate, nor glad,
            shrug on disaster, some force meant

to push them forward (hungry
        for the next taste on the wind, and traveling light,
their duffles and galoshes abandoned with pinched,
        particular lifetimes of advice, suggestions
            taken, still untaken), not to fix them here.

Numbers

They won't stick. They gleam like brilliantine.
Perfect parsers, they jostle into essence
Then reappear, renewed. A trillion seems
Just so many zeroes. Xed-out, they dance,

Uncoupling and recoupling along a line
Hoofing infinite movement, can-can's limber
Leg and best foot forward, tapping time
Until time is up and they're dismembered,

Dead-broke as syntax, clauses so declined
They tick themselves off. It's only beauty—
Perfect measures measuring the mind—
Mind tries to get around. Pen, brush, or flute. The

Equation tooled to figure life. Amount
Imagination multiplies. Takes to account.

Pantoum Unproved

Toni Butler, 1911 – 1998

First, you take leave of your senses.
Then, you lose your mind
to wonder. Split the difference:
what the machine can't count.

When you've lost your mind,
who's left to find you? The clock,
just a machine, can count
but not measure a second.

Who's left? Define *you*. The clock,
strung on a nerve, ends
its first measure, its second.
Every body gives way:

unstrung, unnerved, it ends
in its loss. Embodied,
you give yourself away
bit by bit, fragmented

by losses you embody.
The moment flies apart,
bit off, so fragmented
you must forget you are

a moment flown. Parsed,
wondering, splitting difference,
forget you are yourself
first taken, then left senseless.

Anatomist

The width of the shoulder is 1/4 of the whole. From the joint of the shoulder to the hand is 1/3, from the parting of the lips to below the shoulder-blade is one foot.

—DaVinci's notebooks

And if you should have a love for such things you might be prevented by loathing, and if that did not prevent you, you might be deterred by the fear of living in the night hours in the company of corpses.

—Ibid.

Dawn. Blade's touch, more gentle
than any lover's, which does not consider

limiting damage, lifting only
skin to bare artery, fat from muscle left
intact under eye's dispassion. Only the dead

deserve delicacy. Or stone, against which
chisel tests its measures—

the body flayed.
           Here, I rise through
furrow and light, the swell cut
fringed with oak, sage, grass long declined

yellow, wind's dry caress
under which earth

holds and mountains keep
distance so austerely—
in that clench, slip of skin

over bone the wind makes whistle,
this land, for all
its salt and dry and poison, comes into

itself. Gluteus maximus
knots into the climb, into rectus
abdominus; knees hinge; every stride

the tiny footbones flex—even
shoulder blades move as if to flight detailed
centuries ago, by candlelight,

under hands moving
numerable bones. I could never hold

still in marble readiness,
white muscle keeping action furled to say

here's what stone means, though it's art
making that cut, Thoreau of the body

dividing arm into wrist into torso, multiplied
by head, halved height supplemented by

scrotum's length. Da Vinci's constant:
his body speaks down the centuries,
one, me, magic

number translated into flesh,
then stone. That act withheld
increases power, until

it erodes, the surface
pocked and smoothed, chiseled limbs

blurred, then thinned, then fallen into
such company. Bread, sun,
word, dawn air chilled

by water and midnight's ghost: the lift
of thigh becomes thigh, lung,
and heart, alchemy growing

motion incarnate, blood and flesh
twitching even as the pace winds down.

III. ALCHEMY

Outside Newton's House
April 1999

That's what the alchemists want to do: to turn one element into another.

—Copenhagen

1. Abstract:

Error. Crime. No, make that *trespass.*
Disaster. Redemption. Journey by water.
                                        Brackets:
Two wars. Interval: with goat.

2. Question:

How do we know what we're seeing? What sees us?

3. Problem:

Just staying dry in this country. I'd ridden the train
Through rain- and glass-bent light to find—no bus.
"Come all the way from America to see that house,
Didn't you?" the cabby kept saying.
The truth: not exactly. I'd come from Leeds.
Metered now, counted out, timed back,
I marked the moment cost becomes no object. My luck:
They'd changed the closing day.
                                        What I needed:

My own change. Clothes, fortune, or better, element:
Water to gold, cloud to sun. What Newton
Spent his life's coin looking for. I wasn't
Going to get it, but I had on sneakers and jeans
(Still only damp), and the fence wasn't high.
The old glass was undraped against the eye.

4. Hypothesis:

One does what one can: looks for signs,
A trace of any presence; looks for that tree—
Not the original, but scion of its scion—
Though apples are only a fragrant hope, be-
Draggled by rain, and that delicious fall,
The coming into mind of gravity, a bold
Lie, but lovely, its ripening arc all
Fulfillment, late summer, fields gone gold.

But soldiers marched for, against the crown
Just there, on that highway, and in the cities death
Rode the backs of rats, on human breath.
So he lay here, tucked up and thinking. Newton,

Counting blessings, counting the family sheep,
Dreamed not only spheres, numbers, or light
Divided—spectral day from ghosted night—
But of what's elemental, buried deep

In the bred bone. Could he change his fortune?
In this room I peer at, hands cupped to glass,
He dreams on. Rain trickles down my back, as
Newton paces another afternoon

Brilliant with sun. He's thinking nothing great.
No, that's me. How I meet the goat
(Scion of scion?)—he presses against my jeans,
Expelling rainwater like a goaty sponge.

5. Methodology:

Take what comes. So I pet the goat. And,
Even wet, he has a certain sweetness—
At least of face, its pure demands,
And of soft ear, of vibrato voice.
His song rewards my laying on of hands.
You'd never know there still lies, past that hill,
The highway—now the M2—aroar, driven
Wild by hearts that throb with tested metal;

And, beyond that, across the channel,
Boys urge other engines into flight,
Hardly knowing what they drop, battle
Chaos they rise above. They're so light,
And I'm no longer good at the dire, I find,
Or even the sad, as if all my eye touched
Turned to gold, or to gold's illusion—
And there is no difference, or not much,

Is there? So long as illusion holds.
All that glisters, etcetera, but who knows the real
Nugget we want from any fool's gold?
Or, against the world's blast, Newton's idyll.

6. Experiment:

It turns out the other gate was open.
And the caretaker forgives my nose, pressed
To his personal window, my gaze vexed
By his undergarments, futilely strung

To dry across the kitchen. Not on my
Own account, or even the driver's refrain—
All the way from America, didn't she?—
But Henry is never wrong about a person,

Is he?—and Henry, love being blind,
Bleats his after me. A small test:
To change a goat's heart, to turn a mind
From stubborn gristle into tenderness,

Then walk through wet jockeys into history. Say
It all started here—light, attraction,
Every newfangled idea of heaven—but why
This? The past looks safe: so many turns

To choose from: at Cambridge, skipping all those pages,
Newton writes the protest: *Amicus Plato,*
Amicus Aristoteles magis
Amica veritas.

7. Results:

The caretaker thinks I'm nutso,

But harmless, unlike you, Isaac, you
I hardly dare invoke. All of that
Dark creeping under ceilings, beamed so low
You had to divide light to see it

Enumerated. Outside, it just rains harder
On Mrs. Thatcher's hometown, though her drear
Decade's finally over; this country where
Nothing is original anymore

But everything is accurate. Or
Is it the other way? I can't seem
To come to a conclusion. I've got no quarrel
Against you, though your eye ghosts a gleam

Of the human violence we would perfect
In our century, in a flash of brilliance
To put you to shame, its creators shocked
(Against time, against you, they had no chance)

As God must have been, that morning he came
Face to face with his intent, to find
He'd raised the human, light and air from grime,
And his own explosive longing slipped his mind.

Anatomical Theater

Bologna, Padova

The book of the human body . . . cannot lie.
—Vesalius

1. Padova, 1543

Here, Love, Vesalius memorized lines
Parting skin and fat; laid muscle open,

Fibers feathering, pulling to bone; he steadied
Scalpel under the eyes of students elbowing

For the clearest view. That body was done
With all stages but the last performance

Climaxing, like all love stories, in death.
The theater in walnut not yet built.
It was winter. Outside. Wind on his neck.

He worked fast, bare hands conducting
With measured delicacy, though he loved

Only the body. He played,
His back to the house, teasing notes
From organ and heartstring. Nothing personal,

Just the ache of joints, settled blood—
No formaldehyde, nothing to keep flesh

Firm but the cold. He opened it all himself,
Testing blade against a heart gone

Before the public hanging, the trial—slipped
To hatred, wantonness, mere hunger's sleight

Of hand, the body's dire urgencies
Now also gone. *Exeunt.* Spirit

Whipped. Cast loose. Delivered by what
I can't tell from here. Looking close,

Vesalius sees the heart, its separate chambers.
Executes that cut. Given to

Abandon, the lost beat, he forgets
His audience, what he knows. Won't admit
For years he has imagined the body, new.

2. Bologna

Then, how bodies are translated,
Once they decompose, back into art.
A renaissance: the theatre so figured

Either side of the lectern, carved bodies
Flayed but still lively, leg's jaunty cock

Holding up the surgeon, holding forth,
All in wood: loving cuts

Of muscle, veins' traceries so precise
Each becomes a model of creation

Waiting to be electrified by touch.
The bodies of physicians laid in rows

Regular as blank verse. It took eight years
After the bombs fell to put it right,
I think. The caretaker recites in fast Italian

Translated by gesture, the sweeping arm's
Emotion carrying understanding

The way it does in opera, swelling the heart
With certain knowledge. I still don't know:

Who is the woman in chains? Absent a body
They'd use a manikin, modeled for real,
Eyes wide open. A gentle look

For one laid like a box: breast and stomach
Lifting lidlike to muscle, ribs to viscera.
The organs' jewel compartments. Pudenda

Coyly draped. Head thrown back to hair
Flown in ivory, ivory throat exposed.

3. Padova, 1594

The first indoor performance was Fabrizios.'
Windows plastered over. Musicians sawing

A torchlight serenade. For all that,
Still cold. The body in the kitchen
Undergoing stripping, plucking, as

Any woman's for wedding, or debut. Prepared,
The students lean over rails, tiers
So steep there are no chairs: just their breath

Raising hairs on each other's necks
As they crane over to watch the blade

Pierce the solar plexus. The table set.
A passed flask. A joke under the breath.
They're just kids. That dead weight still

Rising to resist. In the wings,
A pig's corpse understudies the human

In case the church arrives. A trapdoor to the river.
Lookout's cue: *Curtains.* The body falls

Away. Slap and freeze,
As if the corpse could feel one jot of what
We feel for it, vivified. The truth:

I don't even know what *you* feel,
Though your heart sparks mine, and your brain's
Awash in electricity—though I know

Without looking where you stand
In any crowded room. Those old painters

Were right: the halo's a charge
We all carry, invisible

Gift of the body to air. It's almost easier,
Imagining the dead. I keep forgetting

This is a love poem: didn't *we*
Reinvent the heart? The push-me pull-you

Of its muscled art. For you, I'd shed
Any flesh, throw off sparks and flotsam

To star the universe, which wastes nothing,
In which every thing is wasted.

4. Operations

Ten-thousand years BC. A manual drill—
Skull and brain are nerveless, and desperate measures

May call forth more time: its measured breath
Against the breathless dark. A comfort

Just to do something. One skull twice
Trepanned. The first hole healed over

Before it failed.
                          The body is no poem.
Not a painting brushed down in layers

The historian x-rays, meticulous
Lover of image and its ghosts—

Eclipse means *abandonment*—
That figure painted over in the corner

Coming into its own again, bearded
And robed in a crimson that became

The fallen curtain, background for the still life.
Too much like the corpse. Without the heart
The body won't perform. Is not a machine, though

It hides what binds it. What would you do
If the scientist found a way to loose you—

Unknotted from your veins, unclenched from muscle,
The bulk of rib and flesh you hardly notice
Though it turns me with all its force—

And freed you, wheeling, goosey as lost breath
Into the room's scattering of air?

(5. *The Identification of the Remains of St. Anthony;*
Miracle of the Broken Glass

So, even the skull has its halo,
All flesh stripped to blessedness,
Beside which this restored glass
Is magic's performance, though likely, enough

Sleeve to hide anything. Salvation from drowning
Being the Saint's particular trick
(*St. Anthony Revives a Boy Drowned in the Lake*),
Or anything to do with water, contained

(Brought back to life, *a Child Fallen Into a Cauldron*),
And the usual detachments, reattachments.
"Sickness," Havasser said, "is self-destruction."
God is—the only medicine.)

6. Bologna, Santa Domingo.

You're right: I have a gift for Judgment
Days—bored of the quietly sacred, I'm drawn,

Before I'm close enough to see the lines,
To the set piece: Satan on our right
Upstaging Christ and shitting sinners

Already singed by his cosmic heartburn;
His handsome devils hoofed and winging

While cherubs merely hover, still on book.
Evil gets a move on; the good sit around

Looking—what else?—good in their tableaux.
This, too, is technical, in the bone:

Messages transmitted over and over,
A machine for faith. Passion's play running
Two thousand years and counting. It never fails

Its cue to transport. Not to specific awe.
Those wings and lilies. *This* blood. *The human*

Moves me to weep: we beat
Our hearts against a drama we reenact.
Stone, flint, chisel, paint, and gold:

Because our bodies keep remaking us
We may never settle.
                              The judgment is
Oddly literal, and wrong: the poker plunged

Up the rectum emerges at the mouth
(Whether Christ's blood falls upon

The upturned face of John, or a skull
Laid at the cross's base, there's plenty, and boneyards

To spare, and so many axes
Grinding, people forever losing their heads)—

But I've been distracted by mere business,
And such attention,
                      7. such elaboration

Sent Luther over the edge: not only gold,
The vaults that carry the heart up into shadow,

But scenes of wood inlaid, backing the choir,
Whose robes rubbed to glisten the ivory helmets,

Crusaders falling under holy cedars.
A snake twining a cross. Everything frozen
For the curtain's fall.
                  People were starving.
                              This

Still breaks the breath, it's so precise.
What else would you want the dying to know? Folds
In the pasha's cloak. There is blood, drawn

By every chisel stroke: in angel's wing,
In Adam's face, turned from the garden gate's

Opening to the performance of his life;
Blood, the idea entering Mary's mind,

Wings aflutter. *Applause.* The world bathes in it,
And still such flight in human hand

Pulsing with mere blood. I want mind
To play it out: the interval between

Blood and the catching heart, the valve pushed open
And muscle suffused. Pleasure not

Requiring touch to raise it. Mary's pulse
Speeding at conception. The body

Preformed for this determined plot. Mine
Still for yours. It only seems
Like forever. Dear heart, even the holy

Binds each breath into some body
And sends it out again to test the air.

Kepler's Paradoxes

The First. The orderly progress of generations.

Like all infants then, Kepler had
A fifty-fifty chance. Not much else—
the church, studiousness, the brain kindling

Numbers down the past to light the future.
Infection. Cold. Hard travel. Inquisition.
Our luck: a parent outliving a child

Feels like time itself folding backward,
Flame into its tinder. Maureen's brother,
Patrick, broken by the road, his hand

On a machine's wheel. Eye caught
By evening's flame reflected. Mind,
I scarcely knew him. Blood, a shard's

Last light, a copy of Calvin fluttering
Pages against gravel. Word's fire
Turned to stone.

The Second. Harmony in numbers.

That same week, my husband

Bends to his machines, measuring
A child's brain, numbers propagating,

Remaking childish impulse, burning tissue
Onto air the surgeons walk through—

Numbers flickering, lighting capillaries.
The surgeons point to matter they cannot touch,
Hands sweeping virtual lobe, voracious

Fire spreading. As in Edward's brain,
As in my husband's mother's, in Shahid's mother's,

In Shahid's. Too late for Edward.
For both mothers, one survived

By her own mother. For Shahid, surviving
His by so few years. Because these days
We far outlive our infancies, at least

As the numbers go, we hardly bear it.
On this child's brain stem, the tumor burns

Everything she is: name, breath,
Sight, hearing. Mother's touch.
She is four years old. Nothing to do

With truth. I have seen her photo, the virtual
Inside of her brain. The surgeons trace it,

My husband's intimate vision, and later trace
Living tissue with a beam of light

That cuts right through. So close. Only hope:
Eye and hand unwavered by the odds.
The child will die.
                    But not now. Not of this.

The Third. Tubingen in time.

I can walk where Kepler walked, wet stones
Spining a town, its flow of commerce anchored
Either end by history's butt and head,
Castle and university pulling the present's

Length. Which is which? And which the church?
After scholarship, the town's industry
Looks to be spectacles, anything
To unjade the eye. I peer

At timbered houses blurred by rain's
Long quarrel, by time, shutters pulled.
A kind of science: my exhausted looking
Carries me away, where Kepler focused

God's word, or God's reflection wavering
The word of man. Where time
Might open to his gaze. If only words
Would fix themselves. I spend the morning

Peering through shop windows at frames
And lenses I don't need, considering
Aviator, cat-eye, star. Stepping into
Vision might remake me, make me see

The Fourth, Kepler's mind,

Dancing on some ancient,
Theoretical pin; angels; air blown

Open into vista, unrolling hills. The present's
Unrelieved. Between what passes

And what carries on, I'm tired of talking
Always to the dead. Not only Kepler.
The weight of them presses against air

My hand moves right through. Today, fog blurs
Its own glimmering view. My mind

Comes between my mind and what is present.
Time between us. The more there is

The better I can see. Science tells
How eye reflects the world, technologies

Invisible to me. I look and look. Beauty
Tells? Kepler bends to God, given

And replaced by human
Word. Only later, the sky becomes

Everything to him. Extravagant claims.
Impenetrable curve. In what sign
Did he know it all? At what point?

The Fifth. Twelve houses.

So the charts bent him

Down from the actual

Stars eked as hints, out-

Lines figuring us

Through time, that

Mystery. Still draws:

What moves them so? What

Catastrophe shines them on?

His sky the same as this one

Turns out force and line.

His sky spun of numbers

Refigures my mind.

The Sixth. At the center.

What good, knowing? We all die.
Because we can remember, we predict

The past creates the future. There's money in it:
Part of the job, to chart nobility's way

By heaven, which K saw just in passing.
At birth, even the present yawns so wide

Any wrong map will do. So in our time,
A scholar finds K's hand on the wheel

Of an infant lost to history. Nothing
Of sudden, particular loss, the pain that keeps

Mind from seeing. I wouldn't predict
For anything. Nor K. He wanted

A little harmony. *On earth as it is—*
Or, more precisely, the other way.

Such a simple gesture: to move the sun
From the periphery and turn us back

To heaven. Edgy, we spin around,
Bask in light so deep I can reflect

Back onto the moon. Watch the paintings:
In time, focus slips from spotlit manger

To the margin's secondary light;
Not the thing itself, but its projection

Clarified by distance between the two.
So why stand we, gazing up to heaven?

The Seventh. On reflection: *Not so much a painter as a mathematician.*

First I see the swans, then the water.

Then the black swans, a pair, heads craned
As if each watched itself mirror the other

And the stream that mirrors each again.
Try to describe it in numbers. God won't stop
Receding behind signs that multiply,

And He takes it all with Him. Call it gone.
Up close, they are dirty—swans—and mean.

On reflection, they're all grace and perfect line.

The Eighth. Reading the stars.

None of which helps. You might as well
Lower your eyes, read the lights strewn

Across the valley floor, as look for signs
Hurtling overhead. *Not so much*
A painter, though what I see below

Bathes in secondary light, a beauty
So impenetrable it pains me
While the numbers repeat. Harmony everywhere,

At least on the surface. *In harmony,*
Meaning. This he knew. Not what
Meaning *is*. The numbers never got us

Any closer. What they describe,
The hand passes through, and time passes

Relentless through the body. All the time,
Mathematician hears music, and the numbers
Describing that music, perfectly pitched,

Become the ladder Kepler climbed
Bar by bar, trying to reach some heaven—
Or was he scaling heaven down to earth,

Music describing numbers for its descent?
Descant. *The idea.* Mathematician thinks

On earth as it is. On reflection, mystic imagines
Stars that bear us shape us

Not in casting us forth, but in how,
Returning, they draw forth our greatest action.

The Ninth: Weil-der-Stadt. The Inquisition.

An argument over land, milk soured,
A sickened goat: for his mother's burning
At least reasons. Kepler returned
So far. Cast out by the church
To plead with it. All he had escaped.
These timbered houses. The cobbled square
So bathed in mild sunlight I can't imagine
Flame scouring bone. But you can count
The dead at City Hall. Mathematician
Strains at the invisible, numbers so many
Stones across a river. From which his mother
Had sent him to become. Mystic too
Lets numbers take him. He could look
Only into the past to see her burn
Down the present. And his mother staked
Her whole bewildered universe on him,
As he had his on her. Once. A long, dry spell.

The Tenth: His blasphemy his fame.

Oh Shahid. Maureen. Sherlie, Edward,
Patrick. Oh, little girl I'll never know.
We can't stop counting against the odds.
By his timely coming his mother was saved
For her natural death. Which in good time
Also came, and left him well behind.

Middle Ages

[H]istory and biology remember in a way that physics does not.

—Carl Sagan

Simple happiness never was enough
though, some days, I feel full of grace.
Equinox. Trees struggling into leaf
between me and night's sky. My lifted face
and my body's singular potential—
in your hands, I still multiply
beyond my one self, reckless, elemental,
opening on the air. And tonight
I've drunk too much red wine, drunk myself into,
out of, sheer companionability
with you, Love, and these all too profligate stars
still high-riding an ancient wind away. Oh,
far-flung, measurable emptiness. All that we
imagine, standing here, is what we are.

Imagine, standing here, that all we are
is hydrogen and ashflake, swirls of dust
determined long ago, like those stars
overheated by time's courtship, so compressed
they became violence. Imagine that
is not the half of it. From our yard, from
this middle distance, we see only what
looks like passing's muddle. All that time
detail piles up, accumulates
invisibly around sharp pinpricks
of presence: our first touch, grief shining through
years of dark matter illuminated.
The mind gives over simply—doesn't it?—
to the universe, so much larger than it knows.

The universe grows larger. What end we know
flies back to us through space, our instruments
gazing into the past. My mind gives over.
In 997 AD, no one counted
a cesium atom's ticks, years by the thousand—
atomic clocks split hairs, and one millennium's
overlong to wait, though Christ descends a
gaudy, star-struck staircase from the sun
to call the moldering from their graven beds.
They counted births of kings. Another realm
where the stars held sway. Accidents
foretold: plague and famine, fire. Behead
a prince or two, and take the royal helm.
History cannot be left to chance.

Our histories won't leave us, though even chance
fails in the end: this middling skin
you touch until it flares, happenstance
of any small wonder—the leaves' new green,
their little, inexplicable skeletons. Night
unfolds into morning, where this life takes
my every breath away, takes my time,
takes all I've got. It will take more luck
than I have ever had—paper, air
against which even the leaf burns out its life,
lifting like a word which, in a moment,
might even drift this far, might lodge *here*,
beyond time, its slant of tone or light
fixed glinting in a personal firmament.

I can't fix the impersonal firmament,
though my eye still grazes the night sky
for your flickering presence. You were meant
to lodge behind my ribs, to catch my eye.
My promise caught in my throat—remember?—a name
I almost couldn't get out, though I'd rehearsed,
the vow moving my tongue, always the same.
Then, before God and you, I lost our first
married seconds with that word, as if
my eye, rising to your eyes out of habit
still primitive—to place the stars in heaven—
was struck by a new constellation. A leaf
hardening into bone. I knew, Love, that
this wasn't the same old news about the weather.

Not the same old: news about the weather,
satellite pictures rolling across the screen;
not what we can't see but know is there—
the past, microwaves, your breath on my skin.
Not the same old words—*just you, forever*—
whispered between lovers to begin,
or spoken to take back—*I don't, not ever*—
after love's consequence settles in.
But this: what even silence holds between us
shining like a leaf, a touch, an eye
creasing at the corner. We let time pass—
because we mean it, because we have no choice—
as we might let a bus pass us by
just to walk, though that bus is the last.

Just keep walking—this kiss may be the last
time our lips touch—into evening.
The atomic clock flecks time down into dust
so fine it means nothing, but its leaven
will lift us into summer, into all
that heft of heat, before autumn burns
the leaves. It's still almost early. Night falls
under stars that fly toward their return.
And, Love, I'm still given to abstraction,
searching night's sky for any sign
the promise holds. Tomorrow: rain, then rough
scrubbing wind to move the clouds, so fast and
even in dissolution so divine
that happiness must be simple, and enough.

Biographical Note

Currently director of the Creative Writing Program at the University of Utah, Katharine Coles teaches poetry, prose writing, and literature and directs the Utah Symposium in Science and Literature. Recipient of both an Individual Writers Fellowship and a New Forms Project Grant from the National Endowment for the Arts, she has published poetry and prose in such journals as *Poetry, The Paris Review, The Kenyon Review, North American Review,* and *The New Republic. Fault* is her fourth collection of poems; she is also the author of two novels, most recently *Fire Season.*

Printed in the USA
CPSIA information can be obtained
at www.ICGtesting.com
JSHW082223140824
68134JS00015B/708